# A Day in the Life of A Light Bulb

Meg Greve

## CREATING YOUNG NONFICTION READERS

*EZ Readers* offer nonfiction for beginning readers in PreK through first grade, using simple language, clear illustrations, and engaging facts to build vocabulary and confidence.

## TIPS FOR READING NONFICTION WITH BEGINNING READERS

### Talk about Nonfiction

Begin by explaining that nonfiction books give us information that is true. The book will be organized around a specific topic or idea, and we may learn new facts through reading.

### Look at the Parts

Most nonfiction books have helpful features. Our *EZ Readers* include color photographs and graphic aids, a table of contents, a glossary, and an index. Share the purpose of these features with your reader.

### Color Photos and Graphic Aids

A lot of information can be found by "reading" photos, charts, maps, and other graphic aids found within nonfiction texts. Help your reader learn more about the different ways information can be displayed.

### Table of Contents

Located at the front of the book, this list shows the big ideas within the text and the page numbers where they can be found.

### Glossary

Located at the back of the book, the glossary defines key words and phrases that are related to the topic. These words and phrases can be found in the text in colored type.

### Index

Located at the back of the book, an index is an alphabetical list of topics and the page numbers where they can be found.

With a little help and guidance about reading nonfiction, you can feel good about introducing a young reader to the world of *EZ Readers* nonfiction books.

EZ Readers is an imprint of:

Mitchell Lane
PUBLISHERS

2001 SW 31st Avenue
Hallandale, FL 33009
mitchelllanepub.com



First Edition, 2027.

Author: Meg Greve
Designer: Rhea Magaro
Editor: Kim Thompson

Library of Congress Cataloging-in-Publication Data
Title: A Day in the Life of a Light Bulb / by Meg Greve

Description: Hallandale, FL :
Mitchell Lane Publishers, [2027]

Identifiers:
ISBN 979-8-89260-844-2 (library bound)
ISBN 979-8-89260-934-0 (eBook)

Library of Congress Control Number: 2025950867

PHOTO CREDITS
Alamy: hoch2wo, 5, 22; Przemyslaw Ceglarek, 7, 22; amana images inc, 10; Dreamstime: Thorken, 22; Shutterstock: Somchai Som, 1, 22; Mega Pixel, 5; Mariana Serdynska, 8, 22; Kostiantyn Voitenko, 13; JOKE_PHATRAPONG, 14; Lopolo, 17; FamVeld, 18; TommyStockProject, 21; Olena Ivanova, 22.

# Table of Contents

# I Am a Light Bulb

My top is round.

My **base** is narrow.

Inside, I have **LEDs**.

Some bulbs do not have LEDs. They have **filaments**. They use more energy.

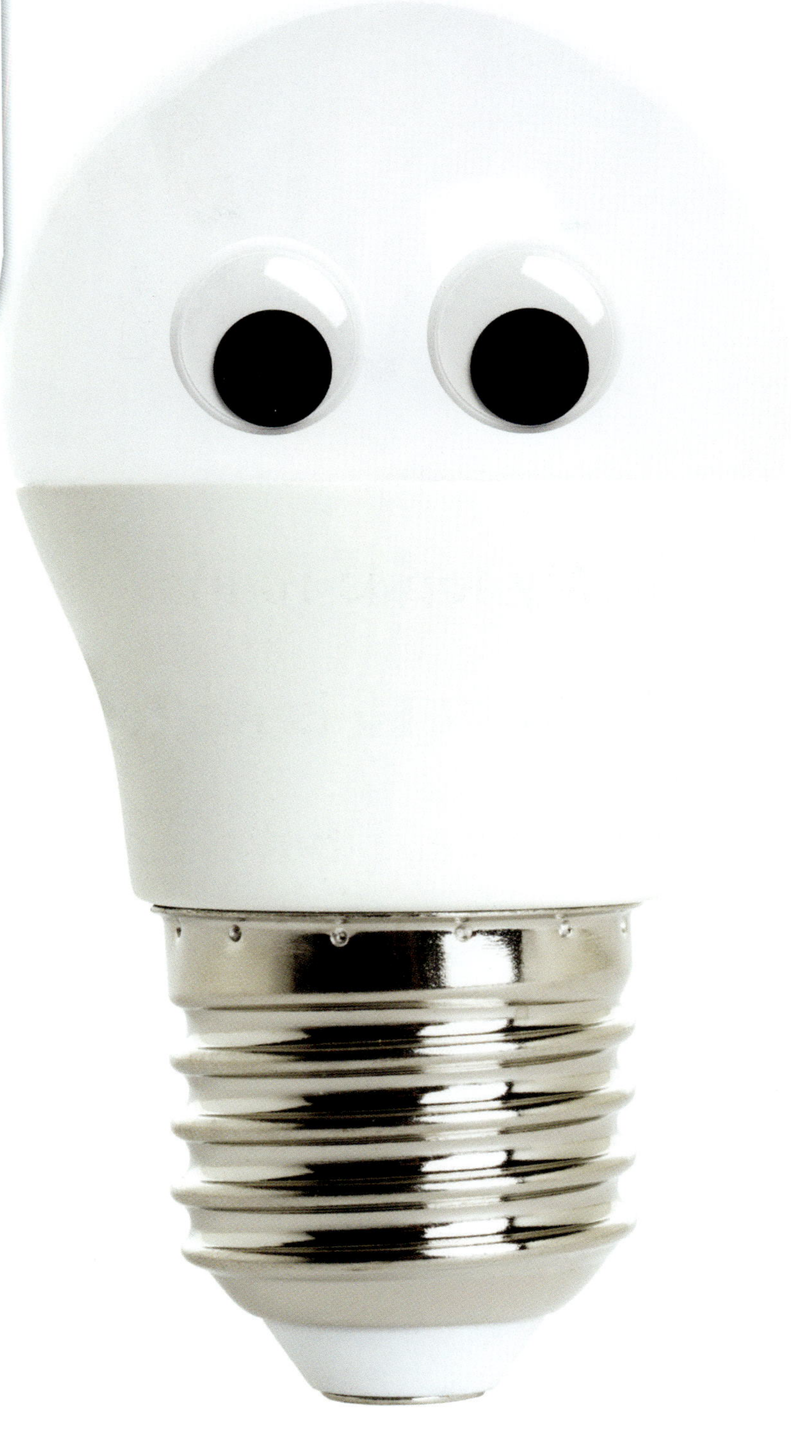

I screw into a lamp.
(Wheee! I love to spin!)

See the cord? Electricity rushes through it.

The flow makes me glow!

A **switch** controls the electricity.

On: Power flows into me. Showtime!

Off: Power cannot reach me. Nap time!

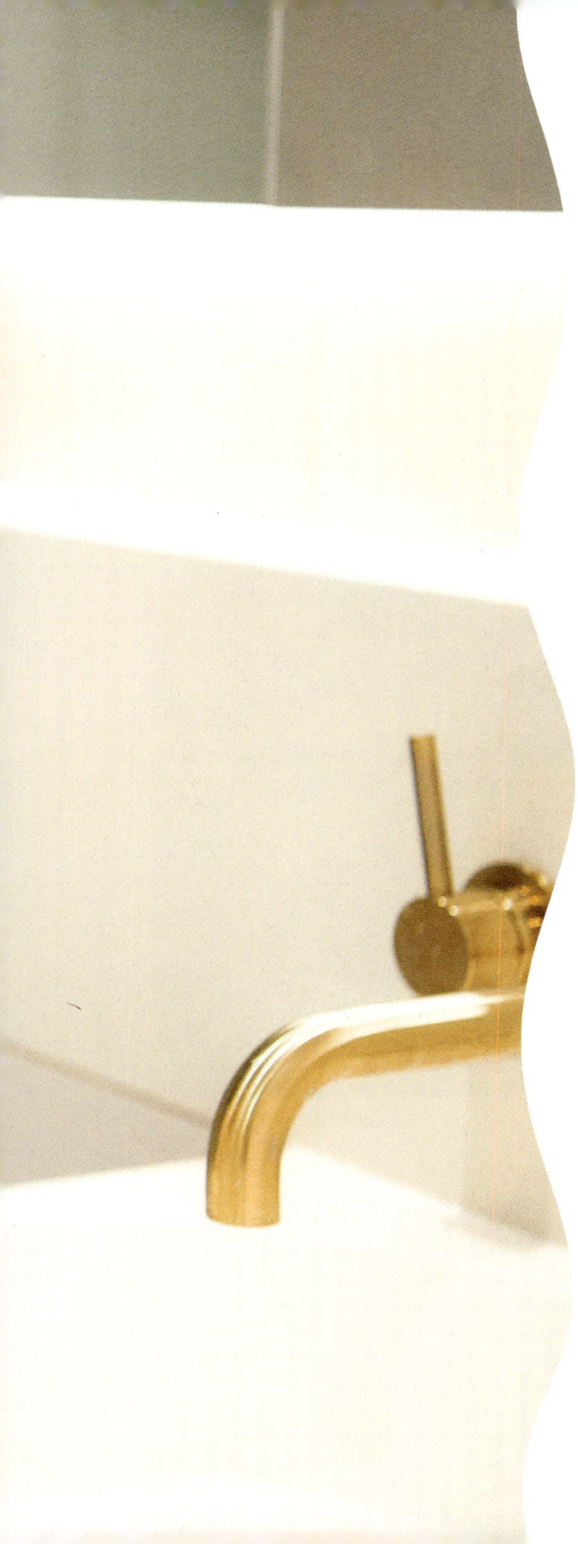

Good morning!

I help you get ready for school.

BY THE WAY...

When you go, please turn me off. This saves electricity.

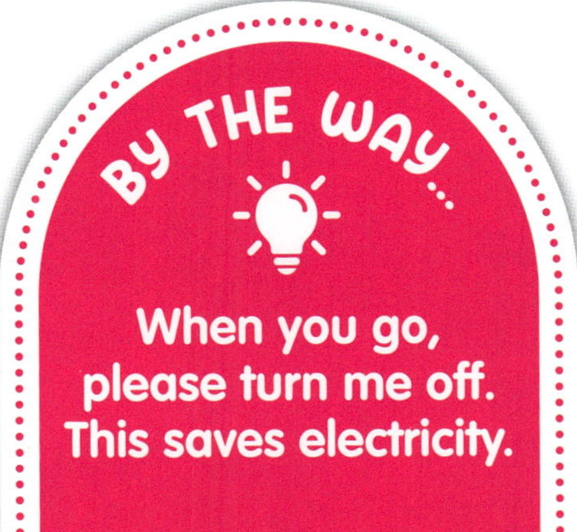

Light bulbs let you see all day.

With us, you can work and play.

BY THE WAY...
We can be different sizes, shapes, and colors for different kinds of lights.

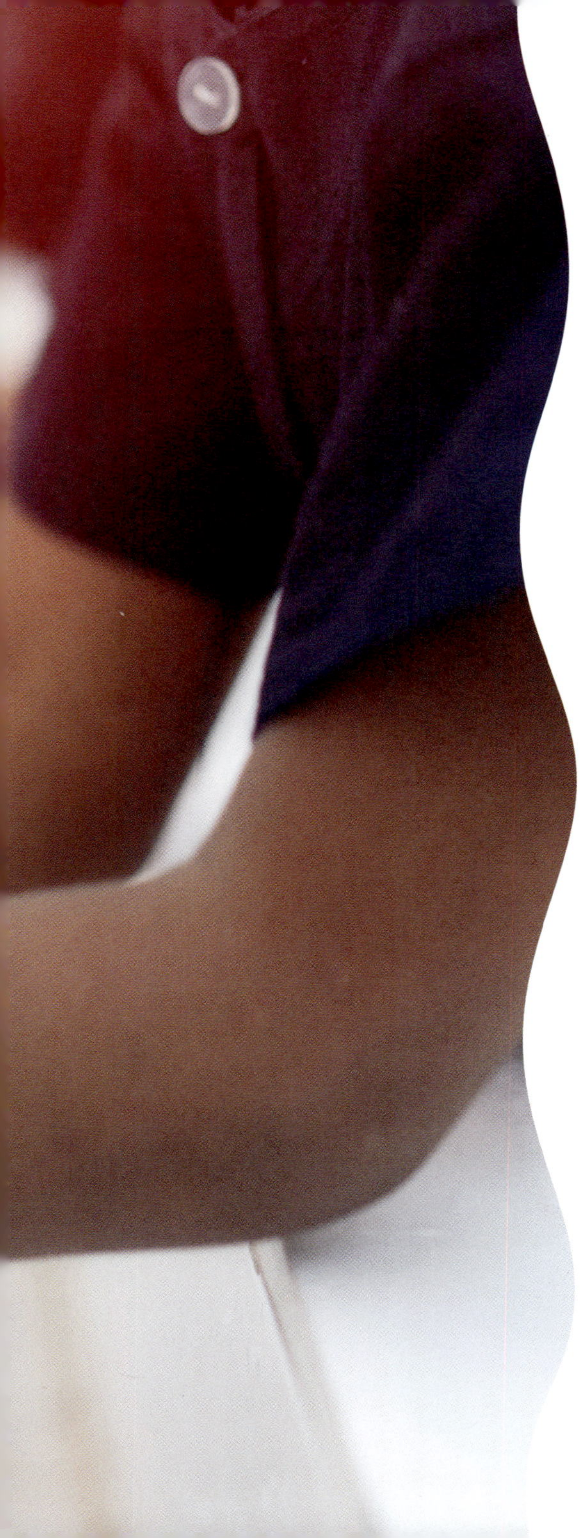

Turn me on in the bathroom.

Turn me off after you wash your hands.

You are home from school. Yay!

I help you find a snack in the **fridge**.

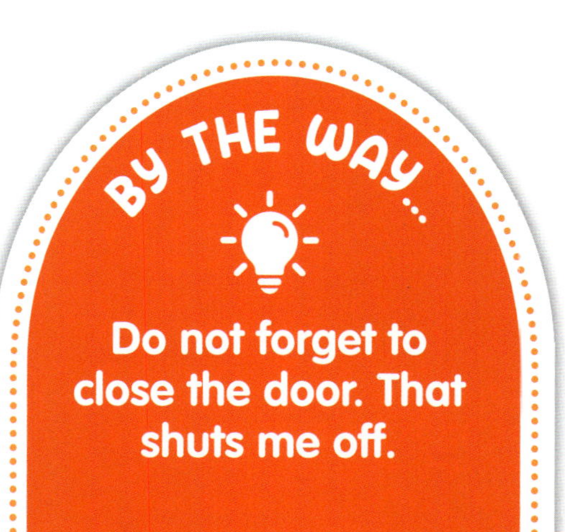

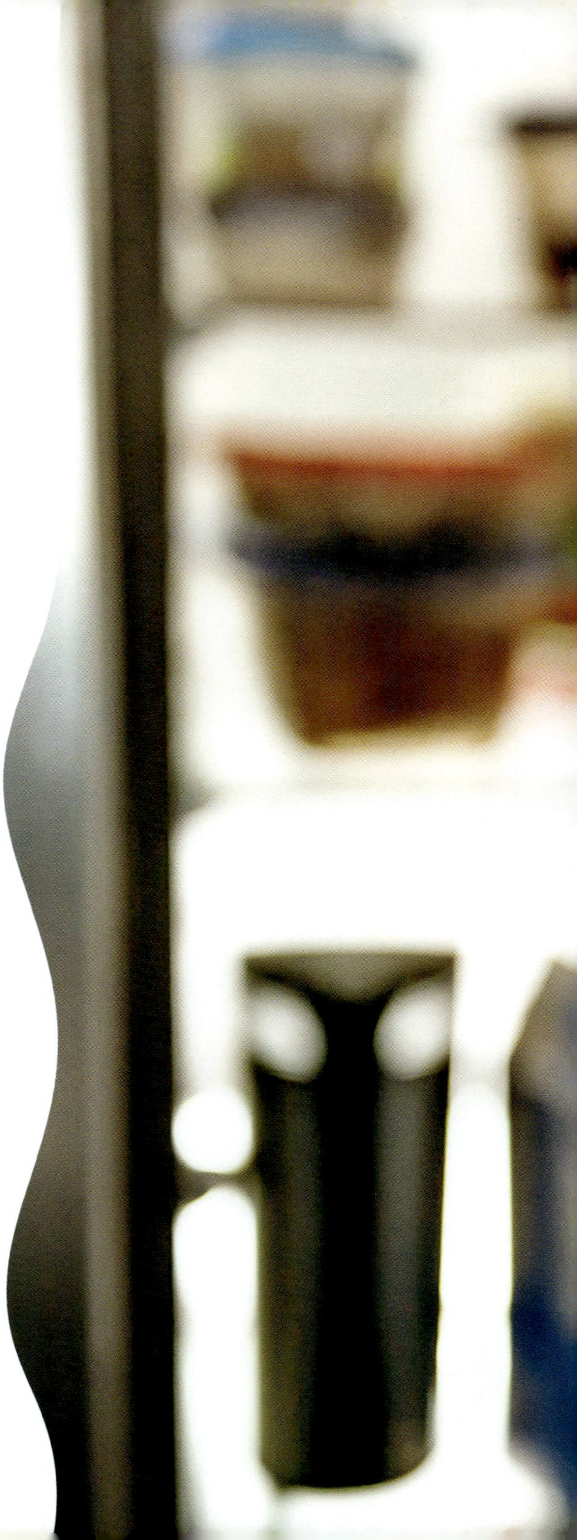

BY THE WAY...

Do not forget to close the door. That shuts me off.

I light up the night.

I love bedtime stories!

BY THE WAY...

Looking at screens at night is not good for you. It makes it hard to fall asleep.

Time to shut your eyes? Shut me off first.

We are both out like a light! (See? I made a joke!)

# Glossary

**base (base)** the lowest or supporting part of something

**cord (kord)** a covered wire that connects an electrical device to an outlet

**electricity (i-lek-TRIS-i-tee)** a form of energy caused by the motion of tiny particles; power that travels through wires

**filaments (FIL-uh-muhnts)** very fine wires; in incandescent light bulbs, filaments glow

**fridge (frig)** short for *refrigerator*; a machine that keeps things cold

**lamp (lamp)** a device that uses a light bulb to give off light

**LEDs (ell-ee-deez)** abbreviation for *light emitting diodes*; electronic devices that light up when electricity flows through them

**switch (swich)** a device that interrupts the flow of electricity in a circuit

# Quiz Me

1. I turn out the lights when I leave a room.

   A. Yes B. No

2. I shut the door after I use the fridge.

   A. Yes B. No

3. I turn the bathroom light off when I am done.

   A. Yes B. No

4. I avoid staying up late looking at screens.

   A. Yes B. No

**ANSWER KEY:**

**How many times did you answer yes?**

4: Awesome! You use electricity responsibly.

3: Great! You are helping the planet.

2: That's okay! Keep learning and practicing.

1: You're starting to learn. Keep trying!

# Further Reading

Amstutz, Lisa J. *10 Ways to Use Less Energy (Simple Steps to Help the Planet).* Capstone Press, 2024.

DK. *All about Light.* DK Children, 2023.

# On the Internet

**SciShow Kids: The Power of Circuits!**
youtube.com/watch?v=HOFp8bHTN30
Learn how electricity makes things work.

**U.S. Energy Information Administration: Energy Kids**
eia.gov/kids/using-and-saving-energy/saving-energy.php
Find tips for saving energy every day.

# Index



# About the Author

Meg Greve has been in education for more than 30 years. She is a mom of two kids who used to leave the lights on all the time. Her favorite kind of light bulb is the one you might find on a Christmas tree!